W9-ABT-765

The Cruelest Place on Earth
Stories from Antarctica

John Nicholson was born in Singapore, and grew up in New Zealand and Australia. He studied and worked as an architect before turning to book design, illustration and writing. He lives with his partner and daughter in a homemade house in the country.

The Cruelest Place on Earth is the product of a long-standing fascination with Antarctica. When John was seven years old, his interest in the continent was sparked by stories of Fuchs and Hillary crossing Antarctica by Sno-cat. Since then he has read everything he could find on the topic.

Other great books in the **True Stories** series:

Bog Bodies
Mummies and Curious Corpses
by Natalie Jane Prior

Monsters
And Creatures of the Night
by Sue Bursztynski

Mysterious Ruins
Lost Cities and Buried Treasure
by Natalie Jane Prior

Potions to Pulsars
Women Doing Science
by Sue Bursztynski

The Cruelest Place on Earth

Stories from Antarctica

John Nicholson

A LITTLE
ARK
BOOK

ALLEN & UNWIN

© text and illustrations, John Nicholson 1994

This book is copyrighted under the Berne Convention.
No reproduction without permission. All rights reserved.

First published in 1994

A Little Ark Book, Allen & Unwin Pty Ltd
Distributed in the U.S.A. by Independent Publishers Group, 814 North Franklin Street,
Chicago, IL. 60610, Phone 312 337 0747, Fax 312 337 5985,
Internet: ipgbook@mcs.com
Distributed in Canada by McClelland & Stewart, 481 University Avenue, Suite 900,
Toronto, ON M5G 2E9, Phone 416 598 1114, Fax 416 598 4002

10 9 8 7 6 5 4 3 2 1

National Library of Australia
Cataloguing-in-Publication data:

Nicholson, John, 1950 – .
    The cruelest place on earth.

    Bibliography.
    Includes index.
    ISBN 1 86448 244 3.

    1. Natural History – Antarctica – Juvenile literature. 2. Environmental protection –
    Antarctica – Juvenile literature. 4. Antarctica - Research – Juvenile literature.
    I. Title. (Series: True stories (St. Leonards, N.S.W.)).

919.89

Designed by Site Design/Illustration, Melbourne
Set in Century Old Style and Helvetica Condensed Light
Printed by McPherson's Printing Group, Victoria

Picture Credits:

Australian Antarctic Division / G. Howarth: 2 / P. Murrell: 6 / A. Nutley: 7 / P. Sprunk: 3 /
Frank Hurley: 1 • Australasian Nature Transparencies / Kelvin Aitken: 4 / Jonathan
Chester: 5
(numbers refer to photographs in the colour section)

Cover image © Australian Antarctic Division / H. Ponting

Thanks to Catherine O'Rourke for assistance with picture research.

Acknowledgment

I am grateful for the help provided by the Australian
Antarctic Division in Hobart.

Contents

Introduction

ANTARCTICA! For one hundred years it has been a
magnet for adventurers, a mystery to scientists, and a
source of fascination for all. The short history of human
beings in this cruelest place on earth is rich in courage,
achievement, adventure and tragedy. But our presence
there has left a legacy of environmental damage that will
take many decades to repair.

This book looks at just some of the
adventures, some of

the practical problems faced by people working there and some of Antartica's idiosyncratic animals. It also examines some of the thorny issues we must face up to when we consider the future of this cold but beautiful place.

Read it from start to finish if you like, or just pick out the chapter that interests you.

1
Antarctic Superlatives

Antarctica is the coldest, windiest, highest, driest, emptiest and most isolated continent on earth.

The coldest continent

Seventy million years ago, Antarctica enjoyed a comfortable semi-tropical climate. Tall forests grew and the strange animals of ancient Gondwanaland ranged over a huge landmass encompassing Antarctica, Africa, India, Australia, and South America.

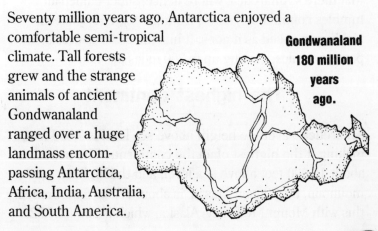

Gondwanaland 180 million years ago.

Sixty million years ago, Australia and New Zealand were the last to split away. Around 25 million years ago, the forests disappeared as snow and ice covered the remaining land.

Today, high on the Antarctic plateau, where even the air freezes into a grey-white mist, the annual mean temperature is −58°F to −76°F. Here, at Russia's Vostok base on 21 July 1983, −128°F was recorded, the lowest temperature ever recorded on earth. Down on the coast the average is a balmier 14°C to −4°F. (about the same as the freezer in your refrigerator at home). Not even the Arctic can compete with these extremes. Antarctica's high altitudes make it by far the coldest place on earth.

The windiest continent

Seafarers call the oceans lying south of latitude 40° the 'roaring forties'. Further south they talk of the 'furious fifties' and further south still, the 'screaming sixties'. After that there's Antarctica, where dense, super-chilled air tumbles continuously down from the high, icy plateau, picking up speed as it goes. It hits the coast as persistent, powerful gales, gusting up to 200 miles per hour.

The highest continent

Antarctica's average height above sea level is 7,550 feet, making it the highest of all the continents. The plateau is about 15,000 feet above sea level, and the highest mountain, the Vinson Massif, is about 17,000 feet. Compare this with Mount McKinley, Alaska, which is about 20,320 feet above sea level, and Mount Everest which is about 29,000 feet high.

The driest continent

The really surprising thing about Antarctica is that it also turns out to be the driest continent, drier even than the Sahara Desert! Its average annual snowfall is equivalent to 5 inches of rain. In some areas, called the dry valleys, no snow or rain has fallen for over two million years! On the high plateau the annual snowfall is equivalent to less than 3 inches of rain. A little more snow falls near the coast.

Most snow seen in the air in Antarctica has been whipped up by the wind.

When a snowflake falls somewhere in the cold, vast interior, it starts a journey to the sea that will take many thousands of years. Gradually, as more snow falls on top, it will turn to ice. This process

The Wright Valley, a dry valley near the Ross Sea

13

goes on continually, building up more and more ice. The Antarctic ice cap has slowly built up to an average thickness of 8,202 feet and contains over 18 million cubic miles of ice. Over 90 per cent of all the world's ice and most of the world's fresh water is here. Should it ever melt, the oceans will rise 200 feet or more. The enormous weight of the ice cap has compressed the rock beneath it, lowering the level of the land by hundreds of feet. Under the pressure of its own weight, the ice slides slowly towards the coast, funneling into rivers of ice called glaciers.

> **Over 90 per cent of all the world's ice and most of the world's fresh water is here. Should it ever melt, the oceans will rise 200 feet or more.**

Glaciers flow towards the sea at a rate of about 33 feet a year. As they grind over rocky irregularities and are forced through narrow valleys, the ice splits and cracks, creating long, deep chasms ranging from just a few feet to 98 feet across. These crevasses are the recurring nightmares of all Antarctic exploration. The largest glacier, the Lambert, is 125 miles wide at its mouth and pushes 22 cubic miles of ice out into the ocean every year.

The ice sliding off the continent forms shelves of floating ice, up to 3,000 feet thick near the land, and tapering to 650 feet thick at the outer edge. This ice is sometimes called 'the barrier' because this is how it appeared to early mariners. It moves up and down with the tides, causing huge crevasses and ridges to form where it is 'hinged' to the land-based ice. At various points the ice shelf is also stuck on pinnacles of rock in the sea. The largest of these shelves, the Ross Ice Shelf, measures nearly 500 miles from the coast to its outer edge and contains 30 per cent of all Antarctic ice.

Great chunks of barrier ice are continually breaking off to form 'tabular' or flat-topped icebergs 600 to 1,000 feet high and many miles long. The largest ever seen was 200 miles long and 60 miles wide. Many icebergs take years to break up and melt, gradually adopting more bizarre and irregular shapes in the process. Icebergs are sometimes called 'floes'.

Sea water, because of its salt content, freezes at a slightly lower temperature than fresh water, forming sea ice. Icebergs of sea ice are much smaller, but it is these which rapidly cover large areas of ocean at the beginning of winter forming the pack-ice. And it is pack-ice that iced in and even crushed many explorers' ships.

The emptiest continent

Not surprisingly, Antarctica contains fewer life forms than any other continent. Only two flowering plants and a number of lichens and mosses are all that remain of Gondwanaland's grand forests. The land-based animals are even rarer: just a few microscopic invertebrates like mites and springtails.

Sea life is much richer. Luxuriant growths of seaweed and algae flourish even under the permanent ice shelves. Animals range from the tiny plankton (microscopic plants and animals) and krill (a small shrimp-like creature) to large seals and whales. Giant squid and 120 of the world's 20,000 species of fish live here too. Sea birds, especially the ubiquitous penguins, are Antarctica's most abundant residents. Many animals have developed unusual ways of surviving in this harsh, cold climate. Fish maintain exceptionally low body temperatures, and other creatures keep their outer bodies at much lower temperatures than their body cores. Penguins and seals have a thick layer of oily blubber under their skin, and this is further insulated with feathers and fur.

There is no history of people living in Antarctica. Only in the last 200 years have visits been made, largely for sealing, whaling and scientific purposes. Today there are 44 permanently occupied bases.

The most isolated continent

No other continent is further away from its nearest neighbors than Antarctica. The southern tip of South America is the closest, 620 miles away across Drake Passage, the stormiest waters in the world. South Georgia Island is 745 miles away.

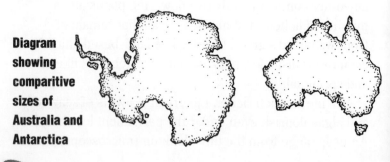

Diagram showing comparitive sizes of Australia and Antarctica

Australia and New Zealand are about 1,550 miles away.

Surrounding Antarctica, the roaring forties, furious fifties, screaming sixties and finally the pack-ice still form a daunting series of obstacles.

Antarctic exploration: the key events

1772–75   Captain James Cook circumnavigates Antarctica, crossing the Antarctic Circle three times in the *Resolution* and traveling further south (to 71° 10') than any before him.

1819–20   Captain Fabian Von Bellingshausen of the Russian Navy is the first to sight the Antarctic continent from his ship the *Vostok*.

1819–20   The sealers Nathaniel Palmer from Connecticut (U.S.A.) and Edward Bransfield, from Britain, also lay eyes on the Antarctic Peninsula just days after Bellingshausen.

1823   Sealer James Weddell, from Britain, discovers the Weddell Sea by going even further south (to 74° 15').

1832   Another British sealer, John Biscoe, circumnavigates Antarctica in the *Tula*.

John Davis, a Yankee sealer, *may* have been the first to set foot on Antarctica.

1839   Dumont D'Urville in the French naval ship *Astrolabe* discovers Adélie Land.

1840   U.S. Navy Captain Charles Wilkes, in the *Vicennes*, discovers and maps a large stretch of coast near the South Pole .

1841   Sir James Clark Ross, with British naval ships *Terror* and *Erebus*, discovers the Ross Sea and Ross Ice Shelf, Victoria Land and Mount Erebus and achieves a new furthest south of 78° 9'.

1886   The Australian Antarctic Exploration Committee is formed.

1895   An Australian expedition led by Henryk Bull and scientist Louis Bernacchi is the first to set foot on Antarctica. Expedition member Carstens Borchgrevink steals the glory by leaping ashore ahead of the others.

1897   A Belgian expedition, led by Lieutenant Adrien de Gerlache in the *Belgica* spends the winter in the pack-ice offshore. One of the expedition members is Roald Amundsen, a man destined for even greater exploits (see chapter 2).

1898–1900   Carstens Borchgrevink returns and is the first to lead an expedition which stays on the Antarctic mainland throughout winter. He sets a new furthest south of 78° 50'.

1901   Dr. Erich Von Drygalski of Germany and Otto Nordenskjold of Sweden lead national expeditions to Antarctica.

1901–2   British Navy Captain Robert Falcon Scott, Ernest Shackleton and others make the first attempt to reach the South Pole in the *Discovery*. They reach 82° 17' south before illness and lack of food forces them to turn back. Also on this expedition is Australian scientist Louis Bernacchi.

1903   Jean-Baptiste Charcot leads a French expedition notable for many advances in clothing and equipment and for its concern for the preservation of Antarctic wildlife.

1907   Ernest Shackleton returns to Antarctica in the *Nimrod*, leading his own expedition which includes Australians Douglas Mawson and Edgeworth David. He establishes a new furthest south of 88° 23', only 60 miles from the South Pole, before turning back. Mawson and David are the first to climb Mount Erebus and to reach the South Magnetic Pole.

1911   Norwegian Arctic explorer Roald Amundsen comes south in the *Fram* and, in a well-organized dash, is the first to the South Pole (see chapter 2).

1911–12   Scott returns to Antarctica and reaches the South Pole only weeks after Amundsen. On their return journey Scott and his four companions all perish (see chapter 2).

1911–14   Douglas Mawson leads an Australian expedition to the South Magnetic Pole and to explore portions of George V Land. Mawson survives a nightmare return journey; his two companions die and all his food is lost (see chapter 4).

1914–17   The Imperial Antarctic Expedition led by Shackleton is stranded on the ice when their ship, the *Endurance*, is hemmed in and crushed (see chapter 4).

1928   Australian aviator Hubert Wilkins makes the first flight over Antarctica.

1929   Richard Byrd (of the U.S. Navy) makes the first flight to the South Pole and back in a three-engined Fokker, the *Floyd Bennett*. He gains sufficient height by throwing all emergency food rations overboard.

1929–31   Douglas Mawson leads a British/Australian/New Zealand expedition to Antarctica.

1934   Richard Byrd winters alone in a small hut making weather observations, almost dying of carbon monoxide fumes from his faulty stove.

1946   The U.S. military's 'Operation High Jump' maps vast areas of Antarctica using aerial photography.

1955–8   New Zealand mountaineer, Sir Edmund Hillary and British explorer, Vivian Fuchs lead a Commonwealth expedition to cross Antarctica using motorized transportation (see chapter 6).

1957–8   U.S. 'Operation Deep Freeze', coinciding with the International Geophysical Year, establishes a permanent base at the South Pole.

2
Amundsen and Scott

The quick and the dead

It is a curious fact of human nature that legends are made out of glorious foul-ups, while patient achievement goes unnoticed and unsung — or is credited to good luck!

Consider the stories of Amundsen and Scott.

Captain Scott

Captain Robert Falcon Scott RN, 'Scott of the Antarctic', or 'The Owner' as the members of his ill-fated second expedition called him, now strides the wintry wilderness of Antarctic myth-ology like a Colossus.

The Cruelest Place on Earth

If you know nothing else about Antarctica, you will probably have heard of Scott's dramatic and tragic journey.

But why? Scott risked and squandered human lives as no expedition leader has, before or since. His expeditions were dogged with fundamental errors of judgement over relatively simple questions, and he failed in his primary goal of being the first person to reach the South Pole. That honor belongs to the lesser known and less glorified Norwegian explorer, Roald Amundsen.

Amundsen was the son of a well-to-do farming family.

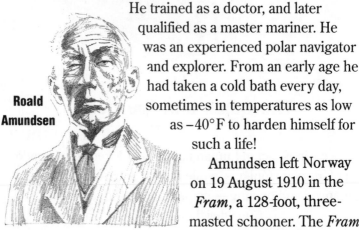

Roald Amundsen

He trained as a doctor, and later qualified as a master mariner. He was an experienced polar navigator and explorer. From an early age he had taken a cold bath every day, sometimes in temperatures as low as −40°F to harden himself for such a life!

Amundsen left Norway on 19 August 1910 in the *Fram*, a 128-foot, three-masted schooner. The *Fram* had been built by Amundsen's mentor, Arctic veteran Fridjoff Nansen, especially for polar exploration. In particular she had an auxiliary diesel engine, requiring less storage space for fuel than conventional coal-fired engines. Amundsen's public intention was to try and reach the North Pole. Soon after his departure, however, he headed south, announcing to the world much later that he would race Scott to the South Pole. It is not clear if this had been his intention all along, or whether the success of the American explorer Peary in reaching the North Pole during 1910 caused his last minute change of mind.

Scott's second Antarctic expedition had sailed from London only seven weeks earlier, on 1 June, in the *Terra Nova*, a 187-foot converted Newfoundland whaler with coal-fired auxiliary engines.

Scott was a talented and hard-working naval officer from a poor naval family. He had no experience of, or interest in, polar exploration, but he regarded leading an Antarctic expedition as the perfect opportunity to further his naval career. He was a disciplinarian, physically strong and fit, with an iron determination—but no sense of humor. He could be charming and friendly, but was subject to moods of severe depression and self-criticism. He brooded endlessly over decisions to be made, did not welcome advice, and would not announce his decisions to others until the last minute. Nonetheless, he was well liked.

The objects of Scott's expedition were wide-ranging. Magnetic, meteorological, and glaciological observations were to be made, and geological and botanical specimens collected. However the primary objective was to carry the British flag to the South Pole. 'The main object of the expedition is to reach the South Pole and secure for the British Empire the honor of that achievement,' said the publicity material distributed at the time.

It was an age of nationalism, when glorious deeds undertaken for your country seemed more worthwhile than they might be considered today. Only a few years later millions of young men from all over the world enthusiastically enlisted to fight and to die in the bloody trenches of Europe in World War I. Against this background we can perhaps better understand the spirit of patriotism which drove both Scott and Amundsen into their dangerous competition.

Scott heard of Amundsen's intentions when the *Terra Nova* docked in Melbourne to take on coal. He was furious. Scott regarded the South Pole as his personal challenge, and the Ross Ice Shelf as his private property. Even fellow countryman Ernest Shackleton had been refused permission to use the hut built during Scott's earlier expedition!

Both expeditions intended to establish bases during the summer of 1910–11, and then wait until the following summer for their journeys to the South Pole.

On the *Terra Nova* were 460 tons of coal, four 'motor-sledges' (a sort of tractor), nineteen Siberian ponies, 33 dogs and provisions, including 162 carcasses of mutton, 3 tons of rice, 5 tons of dog food, 30–40 tons of pony fodder and 35,000 cigars! On 4 January 1911, Scott's men began unloading all this onto the ice near Cape Evans.

On the *Fram*, Amundsen had 97 Greenland huskies, a prefabricated hut and provisions for two years. On 14 January 1911, he and his men arrived at the Bay of Whales, unloaded their supplies and established a base on the ice which they called *Framheim* or 'Forward Home'. From this time on, some important differences in style between the two expeditions start to appear.

Scott's men worked seventeen hours a day, every day, unloading supplies, hauling them over the ice on sledges and establishing a base. Sledging parties then set off immediately to establish a series of supply depots on the barrier.

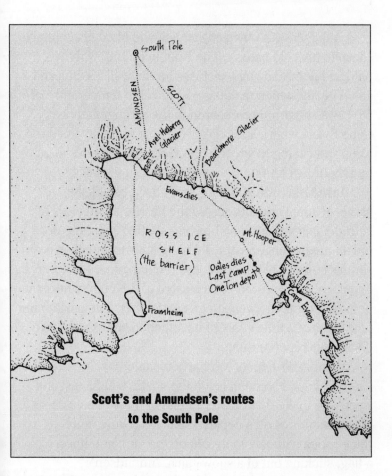

**Scott's and Amundsen's routes
to the South Pole**

On their arrival, Amundsen's men took a day off. They then put the dogs to work hauling equipment and supplies to the proposed base, but continued to have regular days off. Later, during the journey south, 'holidays' were a regular and planned feature of the schedule and were generally spent lying in the tent reading, talking or sleeping. Scott's team never had a day off, unless weather conditions forced them to do so.

The Cruelest Place on Earth

Amundsen was obviously a man who liked his comforts (despite his cold baths!). The Framheim hut, with its polished floor and rugs, pictures on the walls, sauna and an oil heater which maintained a daytime temperature of 68° F, was luxurious compared to the arrangements at Cape Evans where a thin layer of ice perpetually lined the walls and ceiling inside the hut. Even Amundsen's dogs had their own tents!

During that first summer, Amundsen established a series of supply depots across the barrier at intervals of 1° latitude, in a straight line heading south. Again, the dogs did all the hauling. Scott used his ponies to establish a similar number of depots at less regular gaps. The largest depot, called 'One-ton', was located at the point where the ponies became too weak to go any further. The positioning of this depot a little short of its intended site was to have disastrous repercussions.

Amundsen's depots were accompanied by lines of flags extending for several miles to the north, south, east and west—to make them easier to find in the white vastness of the barrier. Scott's depots usually had little more than a stick with an empty can on top, or sometimes a flag, sticking out of a snow cairn. Amundsen's southern-most depot was 200 miles closer to the Pole than Scott's.

Even such mundane matters as lunch arrangements contrasted sharply. While Scott's men pitched tents and retired for a cooked meal, the Norwegians had hot stew from thermos flasks, and then got on with the job.

It is easy, of course, to be wise after the event, to point out the faults of one group and the positive qualities of the other. At the same time, too much has been made of Amundsen's good luck and too little of the sensible and thoughtful planning, no doubt born of experience, which almost guaranteed him success.

The major difference between the two expeditions, and the one which had the most far-reaching effects was, to put it simply — dogs. Amundsen left Norway with ninety-seven, arrived in Antarctica with over a hundred, started for the pole with fifty-two, and took eleven back to Norway for a pampered retirement. The dogs did *all* the sledge-pulling. During the polar trip, as provisions were consumed and the sledge loads lightened, some dogs were slaughtered and their meat became food for the remaining dogs. The men rode for considerable distances on the sledges. At other times they were towed along on skis. They carried nothing themselves.

Scott's plan was to start out with the largely untested motor-sledges, take the ponies across the barrier to the start of the Beardmore Glacier (about halfway), take two dog teams up the glacier, and then rely entirely on man-hauling — that is, the men themselves would be harnessed in front of the sledges to pull them along. The motor-sledges and ponies, however, did not live up to expectations, and man-hauling became the principal means of propulsion for most of the southern journey, and all of the way back.

But all this was still six months away. On 23 April, the pale sun finally set over Antarctica, bringing to an end the sledging activities for the summer of 1911. For now, both expeditions were confined to their huts, except for those hardy individuals who ventured out into the cold darkness for scientific observations or to give the animals exercise.

The winter schedule at Scott's Cape Evans base allowed for an extensive program of work as well as relaxation and recreation.

7 a.m.   Night watchman wakes the cook ('Cook' was a permanent job at Cape Evans, Amundsen's men rotated cooking duties.). The cook stirs up the fire and prepares breakfast.

8 a.m.   Breakfast: oatmeal and fried seal liver.

Washing: before or after breakfast, out in the snow for a quick rub down (water melted from snow is too precious to use for washing).

9.30 a.m.–1 p.m. Work: everyone has duties to perform—measuring and packing rations for the summer, repairing or improving equipment and clothing, making scientific observations, feeding and walking the animals, bringing in snow for melting and collecting fuel for lamps and the fire.

12 noon   Pony feeding time: compressed fodder and snow.

1 p.m.   Lunch: bread, butter, cheese, and jam with tea or cocoa. At meal times Scott sits at the head of the table. The others sit where they please.

2 p.m.–4 p.m. Outside work.

4 p.m.–6.30 p.m. More inside work.

6.30 p.m.   Entertainment: somebody is likely to play the pianola until dinner time.

7 p.m. Dinner: soup; seal, penguin or mutton with canned vegetables, followed by dessert. Lime juice or water to drink (alcohol only on special occasions).

After dinner Relaxation: the men play records, read books, play games (chess, backgammon, checkers). Three times a week there is a talk or lecture. Betting on points of disagreement is very common. Bets are not made in money, but in other, more 'valuable' forms of currency such as tobacco or spare socks (a most valued item).

10 p.m. Most are in bed.

10.30 p.m. Lights out. The nightwatchman stays up all night to tend the fire and look after the scientific instruments.

The race for the pole

The sun next appeared briefly on 23 August, and for both camps preparations for the summer took on a new urgency.

Scott's journey of 870 miles would take him past the depots established the previous year on the barrier, up the Beardmore Glacier, and finally over the plateau to the pole. The final group of four men would be accompanied for most of the way by two support groups of four men each, who would turn back after establishing more food depots on the plateau for Scott's returning party.

Amundsen's journey would be slightly shorter, about 800 miles, going across the barrier, up an unknown glacier which he hoped to discover, and from there to the pole. There were five men in his party, with four sledges, but no supporting groups.

Amundsen's team got away first, on 19 October, covering 17 miles on the first day. They traveled light, the men riding on the sledges to the 80° depot where all the equipment for the journey was waiting. Here they spent a day loading up with provisions for 90 days, enough to get them to the pole, then back to Framheim if necessary. From here on they built a snow cairn every 5 miles to guide their return journey. They continued to depot food every 1° until they reached the end of the ice shelf and the beginning of the land. Then they struck their first major problem. Amundsen's hoped-for glacier was certainly there, but the way onto it was blocked by a 90-foot high ice-cliff (about as high as a ten-storey building). Eventually the team scaled the cliff, pulling all the equipment, provisions, sledges and dogs up as well! Two days later they were at the top of the Axel Heiberg Glacier.

Meanwhile the British juggernaut had got underway on 24 October. Two motor-sledges rumbled out of Cape Evans at 1 mile an hour. One broke down almost immediately, the other managed to go about 30 miles. The unhappy drivers unhooked the sledges and started man-hauling.

A week later the ponies followed with more sledges. The ponies lasted longer than the machines, but as they weakened they were killed, the first one on 24 November, a few days past One-ton depot.

By this time the Norwegians were already on the plateau, but had been confined to their tents by a blizzard for four days. Now they pressed on rapidly, reaching the South Pole on 14 December. They stayed three days, then turned for home with two sledges and eighteen dogs.

Scott suffered his first serious blizzard on 5 December, at the foot of the Beardmore Glacier, holding him up for nearly four days. On 9 December he killed the last of the ponies, and two days later the dog teams were sent back to base. From then on Scott's men depended on their own strength and determination to make progress, and to survive. They had to climb nearly 10,000 feet up the Beardmore Glacier and then onto the bitter Antarctic plateau. On 13 December, the day before Amundsen reached the Pole, they managed only 4 miles.

On 9 December he killed the last of the ponies, and two days later the dog teams were sent back to base.

On 21 December, the first support group turned back. On 30 December, the biggest and strongest member of the party, Petty Officer Edgar Evans, cut his hand badly while replacing sledge-runners. The wound failed to heal, probably due to dietary deficiencies, and became a severe handicap for him and his companions. The following day four sets of skis were left behind for the last support party to pick up and use on their return trip. Scott decided that they would not be needed again before the support party turned back several days later. This was true, but at the last moment he decided to take an extra man with him to the pole, and send only three men back. This man, Lieutenant 'Birdie' Bowers, was therefore without skis and had to struggle on through 170 miles of deep snow while the others skied. The decision to take an extra man to the pole created a whole series of serious, yet quite foreseeable problems. Five men now had to sleep in a tent designed for four and the cooking equipment designed to heat four saucepans of food at once now had to cater for an extra meal. Cooking consequently took half an hour longer at every meal, and of course more fuel (kerosene) was used.

Quantities of food and kerosene for the journey had been worked out very carefully. Every pound counted, and provisions left at depots along the way were only just sufficient to see the polar party home — as long as nothing went wrong. Later, when Scott found that some of the paraffin in several depots had leaked, he must have regretted the extra cooking time necessitated by taking that extra man to the pole.

Ten weeks of unremitting struggle, lack of rest and inadequate food were now starting to take their toll. On 10 January 1912, for example they only managed 6 miles, 'but at fearful cost to ourselves', Scott's diary records. This was despite having just had two days rest forced on them by blizzard conditions.

The eyes can play strange tricks in the uniform whiteness of Antarctica. What looks like a range of rocky mountains in the distance can turn out to be a pile of horse droppings just ten 30 feet away. A tin can left in the snow might easily be an enormous water tank. But when a line of black flags loomed up out of the haze on 16 January, there was no room for misinterpretation. The game was up. The race was run — and lost. Scott and his companions reached the Pole the following day, one month and four days too late. They were weak, disillusioned, and feeling the intense cold much more than they expected. 'Great God!' wrote Scott, 'This is an awful place.'

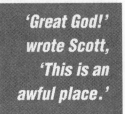

'Great God!' wrote Scott, 'This is an awful place.'

A week later on 25 January, Amundsen and his four companions, still traveling well and with plenty of food, got back to Framheim. The whole journey had taken them 99 days. On their way south, Amundsen had planted frozen fish in the snow, tails exposed, at regular intervals to keep up the dogs' enthusiasm on their way back!

With a minimum of ceremony, Scott's men headed for home. The relentless southerly wind now blew at their backs so they hoisted a sail and, as Bowers records, 'fairly slithered along'. For three weeks they pegged away the miles, making good progress to the top of the glacier despite Evans's worsening physical and mental state. Titus Oates, the taciturn army officer whose main responsibility had been caring for the ponies, was now suffering severe frostbite, and Scott and Evans had fallen into a crevasse, their rescue only adding to the team's problems. Dr Bill Wilson, the other member of the party, strained a leg tendon and suffered a bad case of snow blindness.

On 7 February they reached the top of the glacier, celebrating the event with a rock-collecting expedition. Thirty-five pounds of samples went onto the sledge, to be dragged on and on by the exhausted men, right to the bitter end. How could they have been so stubborn? Was this a last minute attempt to beef up the scientific achievements of the expedition in response to their disappointment at the pole? Why did the supporting parties not collect and carry these samples on *their* way home? They were fresher men with a much easier task to get home before winter.

On 16 February Evans collapsed. He had been having trouble with the adjustment of his boots, and several times had stopped to retie them. Each time the whole party was held up. Eventually Scott told him to stop, fix them properly, then catch up with the others. Later, when Evans failed to follow them, they went back and found him on his knees in the snow, slurring his speech and staring blankly. They put him on the sledge and carried him to the tent in a coma. That night he died.

Evans was the biggest man in the group, but had only been allowed the same amount of food as everyone else. He had been slowly starving for some time, but the final cause of his death was probably a brain haemorrhage. The early stages of scurvy (vitamin-C deficiency) weaken the blood vessels, and he may have hit his head when he fell over on that last day, causing a blood vessel to burst.

For the others Evans's death was a chance to make better progress. He had lagged behind, and towards the end had been unable to pull the sledge or help with the tent. Now they could get ahead, and add his share of food to their own.

But now the whole party was suffering the symptoms of starvation. Oates, with his frostbitten feet, had been marching along in silent agony, and soon he too became a burden to his companions. The shortage of kerosene at many of the depots meant that the men often went without a cooked meal. Their weakened state and steadily worsening health hampered progress so that rations had to last even longer between depots. They became weaker, and covered less ground each day. This vicious cycle continued.

On 9 March, the four men reached Mount Hooper depot, 70 miles from the well-stocked One-ton depot. Scott's diary reveals that he hoped to meet the dog teams here, even though he had given clear instructions that no attempt should be made to come out and meet the returning polar party.

They were now in deep trouble: Oates was near death, kerosene supplies were again unaccountably low, and they were all suffering from frostbite, scurvy, snow blindness and various injuries.

> *Just getting footwear on to their frostbitten feet each morning was taking hours.*

Just getting footwear on to their frostbitten feet each morning was taking hours.

Oates knew he was holding the party up, and said so. What should he do? On 16 or 17 March (the passage of time was becoming blurred) he asked to be left behind in his sleeping bag. Scott would not hear of it, so Oates struggled on. The medical box contained lethal doses of drugs, but the following morning the sick man chose a different end. As a howling blizzard battered the tent Oates uttered those now-famous words, 'I am just going outside, and may be some time.' He stumbled out into the whiteness, and was never seen again.

Scott, Bowers and Wilson discarded Oates's sleeping

bag, a camera and various scientific instruments and plodded on. On 19 March, Scott wrote in his diary, 'Amputation is the least I can hope for now.'

Two days later the men set up camp with enormous difficulty — for the last time. They had enough food for two days, no kerosene, and only ten miles to go to One-ton depot. The next day a furious blizzard began. Further progress, even for fit men, was completely out of the question. They eked out their remaining rations, Scott continued to write in his diary, and the blizzard blew on, day after day after day.

Scott's last diary entry was made on 29 March. Bowers and Wilson were now dead. Scott's rotting feet must have been causing him the most ghastly agony. But he continued to write letters to his family and friends, to his companions' closest relatives and to the general public. He finished, most lucidly, with these remarkably poetic words:

'Had we lived, I should have had a tale to tell of the hardihood, endurance, and courage of my companions which would have stirred the heart of every Englishman. These rough notes and our dead bodies must tell the tale, but surely, surely a great rich country like ours will see that those who are dependent on us are properly provided for. '
R. Scott.

Another bitter winter closed in around the lonely tent.

Back at Cape Evans the exhausted support parties had straggled in. Lieutenant Edward Evans, one of the last group to turn back, was suffering advanced stages of scurvy, and was saved only by the efforts of his companion Thomas Crean. Leaving Evans in the tent, Crean had set off alone to walk the remaining 30 miles with a small amount of food and no tent. A blizzard or crevasse would have killed him and he could not risk stopping to rest. He survived the ordeal, and a dog team was sent out for Evans, who also survived.

Another group, the 'Northern Party', also failed to return to Cape Evans from exploratory work along the coast. They survived the winter by building a snow cave and eating seal-meat, cooked on an improvised blubber stove.

> **They survived the winter by building a snow cave and eating seal-meat, cooked on an improvised blubber stove.**

The following spring preparations were made to search, right up to the plateau if necessary, for the remains of the polar explorers. The search parties would again need an elaborate series of depots and support groups.

As it turned out, such arrangements were not required. On 12 November they found Scott's tent still standing. Bowers and Wilson had obviously died quietly in their sleeping bags. Scott, half out of his, his arms stretched violently across his companions, had had a harder time of it.

Outside the tent, the snow-covered sledge still carried 35 pounds of geological samples.

3
Killer whales and whale killers

Returning from an expedition the summer before
Scott's tragic dash for the South Pole, 'Birdie' Bowers,
Apsley Cherry-Garrard and Thomas Crean had to travel
through an area of pack ice which was beginning to
break up. They camped one night on a portion of ice which
later split off and drifted away. The following day a group
of killer whales approached and began systematically
rocking the floe. They reared up out of the water in unison,
then landed on one edge of the ice. Repeating this action
over and over they set up a rocking motion which
threatened to tip the three men into the water. Eventually
the men scrambled to safety, and lived to tell this
extraordinary tale of planned, cooperative animal
behavior.

Killer whales (or *orcas*) are among the largest of the
cetaceans, the order of marine mammals which also

includes dolphins and whales. Males can grow to 30 feet in length and up to eight tons in weight, while the females are a little smaller. They are highly social animals, traveling and hunting in well-defined groups (or pods).

Killer whale (Orca)

They have a startling jet-black and snow-white coloring and a fearsome array of teeth. Their tastes range from fish, sharks and squid to seals and other whales. They are particularly fond of the limp, jelly-like tongues of large whales. The stomach of one killer whale was found to contain thirteen porpoises and fourteen seals!

There are many stories, similar to that of the explorers on the ice floe, which tell of the orcas' abilities to work together and plan ahead. Whole pods will surround a school of fish, herding them into a smaller and smaller area, often against a cliff or beach. Then, at their leisure, they catch the fish and eat them.

Another story was told during Scott's expedition by photographer Herbert Ponting. Ponting wanted to take pictures of eight killer whales patrolling the edge of the ice shelf. As he stood focusing his camera, Ponting felt a tremendous jolt beneath his feet. One of the killers had rammed the underside of the ice and, as the other seven lined up along the edge, the ice split and cracked around him. Ponting managed to escape by jumping from one fragment to another, but the orcas continued to ram and rock the ice fragments as he scrambled to safety.

Another story is even more striking for the level of planning and cooperation it reveals. Four biologists

Blue whale

working in the Gerlache
Strait saw seven orcas approaching an ice floe on which a
crab-eater seal was sitting. At first one or the other
occasionally popped its head up to look at the seal. They
circled the floe for a minute or two, continuing their
observations. Then they retired a short distance and,
turning, they charged at the floe all in a line. As they
approached they rose as one from the water, then dived
beneath the ice, sending up a wave large enough to tilt the
floe and wash the seal into the sea, where they devoured it.

Blue whales

Whales are closely related to orcas, and both are classified
by marine scientists as cetaceans. Most species of large
whales and some of the smaller ones occupy Antarctic
waters for at least part of the year. The biggest of these,
indeed the biggest animal of any description to have lived
on earth is the blue whale. At lengths up to, and sometimes
over, 100 feet, and
weighing up to 200
tons, blue whales
are bigger even than
the biggest
dinosaurs. The
largest land animal
today is the African

The Antarctic krill

elephant, which weighs in at a maximum of ten tons.

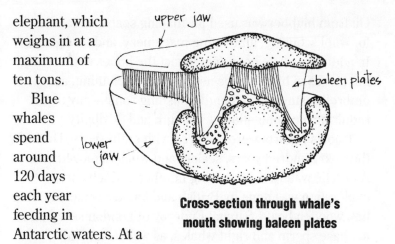

Cross-section through whale's mouth showing baleen plates

Blue whales spend around 120 days each year feeding in Antarctic waters. At a single gulp they take in 60 tons of sea water and then force it out through a fine grille of bony, triangular fins called *baleen plates* which hang from the upper jaw. The baleen plates trap krill and plankton which the whale then swallows. Blue whales have between 540 and 790 baleen plates, the biggest being about 4 foot long. A 150-ton whale consumes three tons of Antarctic krill every 24 hours.

Blue whales feed in the Antarctic but head for warmer waters to breed and give birth. A baby blue whale drinks up to 13 gallons of its mother's milk every day.

Whaling

When James Cook returned from his search for the southern continent in 1775, he reported an abundance of whales and seals in Antarctic waters. At that time, petrol and oil as we know them did not exist, and the thick oily blubber of Antarctic and Arctic animals was highly valued.

Oil from blubber was used for making soap and candles, for wool scouring, lubricating machinery, and for lighting. In addition, whale-bone (not in fact the bones of the whale, but pieces of baleen) was used to stiffen clothing, as umbrellas stays, whip handles, fishing rods—any object requiring a combination of strength and flexibility.

Cook's reports were received with enthusiasm. During the next hundred years, sealers and whalers moved into Antarctic waters in increasing numbers. Much early exploration was done by British and Yankee sealers in their tiny wooden boats. Samual Enderby of London sent fleets to chase sperm and right whales, as well as fur and elephant seals. Edward Bransfield, Nathaniel Palmer, John Davis and John Biscoe were some who sailed south in search of seals, and ended up getting their names permanently on the map.

The first whales hunted, called right whales, were slow-moving, passive and thickly covered with valuable blubber. They provided the whalers with the maximum return for the minimum of work and danger. By about 1900 these whales had almost been reduced to extinction. Antarctic waters, however, were still teeming

Southern right whale

with whales and the bloodiest era of whaling was set to begin. Carl Anton Larsen, a member of the 1901–3 Swedish Antarctic expedition, set up a whaling station at Grytviken on South Georgia island in 1904. That year his whalers caught 183 whales, mainly humpbacks. In 1905, 399 were taken. By 1913 there were six land-based whaling operations in the area, with 21 factory ships and 62 catchers. By then the annual kill was over 10,000.

For a while the whale kills were controlled by the Governor of the British Falklands, Sir William Allardyce, but not for long. With the introduction of stern-slip factory ships in 1925, the whalers began to simply ignore government regulations.

**Humpback
whale**

They ripped through one species after another with alarming swiftness. In 1931–41 factory ships killed 37,500 whales, and the carnage continued at around this level for the next twenty years.

With the disappearance of right whales, whalers turned their attention to the humpbacks. Humpback whales grow to about 60 feet long, and their most startling accomplishment is their singing! Plaintive and haunting sounds, audible underwater for about 20 miles, are arranged in a series of precise songs with a fixed sequence and duration of notes. All the males within a certain locality know and sing the same songs. If interrupted, they will come back to the song where they left off to complete it.

The whalers had slaughtered almost all humpbacks within a few decades. They then turned to the mighty blue whales, but as their numbers began to dwindle in the

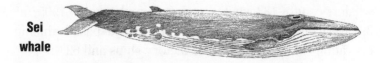

Sei whale

1950s, fin whales were targeted.
Then it was the sperm whales' turn. Sei whales were favored in the 1970s, minke whales in the 1980s.

The most famous fictional whale of all was a sperm whale: the great white whale 'Moby Dick', described in Herman Melville's book of the same name. In his long and spirited war with the whalers, Moby Dick sinks many boats, kills many men, and carries many broken harpoons around, embedded in his massive body. His meanness and obsession is matched only by that of his tormentor, Captain Ahab.

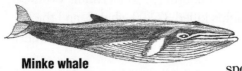

Minke whale

In real life the most bizarre characteristic of sperm whales is their huge square head, containing 2.5 tons of a clear straw-coloured waxy oil called *spermacetti*. Scientists believe that a sperm whale controls the density of its spermacetti in order to alter its buoyancy. Sperm whales can dive to extraordinary depths—up to 4,000 feet—and return to the surface in almost exactly the same spot. Their buoyancy control allows them to simply drop like a stone to the bottom, then return to the surface like an inflated ball.

It is during these forays to the ocean's depths that sperm whales fight their epic battles with giant squid. These 48-foot-long monsters are in reality no match for sperm whales,

Sperm whale

although the whales often carry scars from these encounters. Squids are the least of their worries, however; in 1962–3, 5,773 sperm whales were killed.

Since 1946 when the International Whaling Commission was formed, many countries have tried to curb this terrible slaughter. All too often, however, the commission was made up of members from non-whaling nations. Whaling nations did not join, and so did not consider themselves bound by the commission's kill-quotas. In 1982 whaling was banned altogether, but even then countries like Japan, Norway and Iceland continued to kill minke whales for 'scientific' purposes. Whale meat continues to be sold for human consumption in Japan.

On 26 May 1994 the International Whaling Commission agreed to create a sanctuary for whales in Antarctic waters. All waters south of 40°S are now off-limits to whalers.

Meanwhile, the blue-whale population stands at less than 1 per cent of its pre-whaling level. Humpback numbers stand at 3 per cent, and fin whale numbers are 20 per cent of their pre-whaling numbers. In the absence of so many of the great whales, their food supply has been hijacked by increasing numbers of penguins and seals. Whales must now compete with these newcomers for food, so a return to their previous numbers is unlikely. The survival of the blue whale still hangs in the balance.

Fin whale

4
Mawson and Shackleton

Triumphs of the human spirit

Late at night on 10 May 1916, high in the unexplored
snow-covered mountains of South Georgia Island, three
men were bound on a desperate mission: to reach the
safety of a whaling station at Leith Harbour, on the other
side of the island. They had left three companions,
exhausted and seriously ill, on a windswept southern
beach. Another much larger group was stranded on
Elephant Island almost 800 miles further south.

After fourteen days in an open boat crossing the worst
stretch of ocean imaginable, the three men had still not
rested. They had climbed all day. They were turned back
twice by impassable cliffs and now, at about 7,000 feet,
their path was blocked by an enormous chasm which
stretched in both directions as far as the eye could see.

Time was running out. The weather was closing in. They decided to risk everything on a dangerous strategy. They coiled their climbing ropes into a makeshift three-person toboggan, sat on it one behind the other, and launched themselves headlong into the darkening void. Down, down, down they plummeted, screaming in terror. The thrilling, heart-stopping seconds turned into minutes as they plunged into oblivion. Finally their pace slackened then slowed, and they plowed into a drift of soft snow, exhilarated, breathless, and unharmed. They had made it!

The leader of these three men was Ernest Shackleton, one of the bravest, most reliable and safety-conscious of Antarctic explorers. He had learned the tobogganing trick during an earlier expedition from an Australian geologist. The Australian had used it to swoop down from the top of Mount Erebus. His name was Douglas Mawson.

This chapter tells two stories of spectacular courage and determination shown by these most remarkable men, Mawson and Shackleton.

Mawson

Mawson was a member of Shackleton's 1907–9 *Nimrod* expedition. He and three others were the first to climb Mount Erebus, and later they were the first to toil across the 1,260 miles to the South (Magnetic) Pole. Shackleton himself made it to within 110 miles of

Douglas Mawson

the South (Geographic) Pole, but with dwindling supplies, he and his exhausted team turned back — and survived.

The *Nimrod* expedition had whetted Mawson's appetite to lead his own scientific expedition to Antarctica, and early in 1911 the Australian Antarctic expedition set sail in the *Aurora* with Douglas Mawson as its leader. The main objective was to explore the area surrounding the South Magnetic Pole.

Mawson's group landed near Cape Denison in Commonwealth Bay, directly south of Australia. They built a stout timber hut complete with stove, bunks, a darkroom, workshop, observatory and storage areas (see chapter 5). The *Aurora* sailed for home and they battened down for winter in the windiest place on earth.

When summer came they made a pathway up the ice-cliffs behind the hut. At the top they dug out a cave in the ice, and filled it with food and equipment. This was to be used by sledging parties when they returned from exploratory trips.

On Sunday 10 November 1911 Mawson set off for a nine-week trek with seventeen dogs, three sledges, 1,750 pounds of supplies and two companions. One was Doctor Xavier Mertz, a law graduate from Basel in Switzerland, an experienced mountaineer and champion skier. He was twenty-eight. The other was Lieutenant Belgrave Ninnis of the British Royal Fusiliers, the son of a London doctor and a lover of animals. He was the baby of the group, and he looked so young that the others nicknamed him 'cherub'. Mawson himself was thirty.

They trekked eastwards along the coast from Cape Denison, crossing a large snow-covered dome of ice and

1. Shackleton's ship, *The Endurance*, was frozen solid for eleven months before the pressure of the ice cracked the hull and caused it to sink.

2. Mawson's hut still stands today in the cold wilderness of Antarctica nearly 90 years after it was built.

3. Although cold and cruel, the Antarctic can also be very beautiful, as shown by these magnificent icebergs.

4. This humpback whale calf will grow to about 60 feet long and will develop a wonderful ability to sing. The songs of the adult males can be heard underwater for many miles.

5. The garbage dump at the Mawson Base is an ugly reminder of the human impact on the environment.

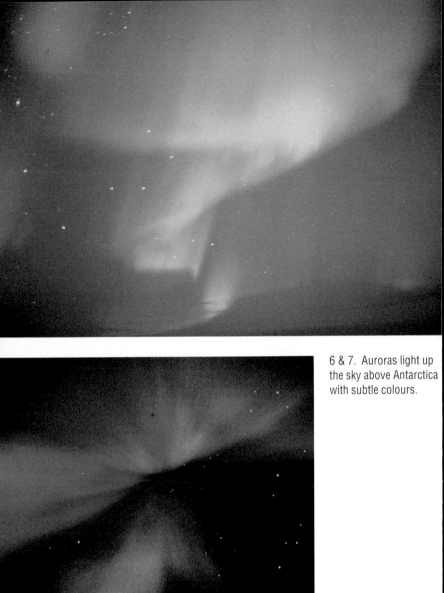

6 & 7. Auroras light up the sky above Antarctica with subtle colours.

then two enormous glaciers—12-mile-wide wide rivers of ice, slashed with deep crevasses. (Later Mawson named these glaciers after his two companions.) They hoped to travel about 15 miles a day, but after five weeks of harsh ice conditions and fearful weather they were only covering about 9 miles each day. With both time and strength running out, Mawson decided to abandon one sledge and push on for one last week before turning back. But on 14 December, disaster struck.

Mertz was in front, on foot, scouting the way ahead. Mawson was next, riding on the first sledge and attending to his scientific records, while Ninnis, nursing a badly infected finger, was behind on the second sledge. It was a fine, calm day and only the panting of the dogs and the swish of the sledge-runners disturbed the peace.

Something, perhaps a slight breath of wind or a change of pace, made Mawson look up. He looked ahead to where Mertz had stopped in his tracks and was staring back, past Mawson, with a curious look of foreboding on his face. Mawson turned to look back, back along Mertz's tracks, back along the tracks of his own sledge to...nothing. No second dog team labored over the snow; there was no sledge and no Ninnis.

Both men ran back along the track to the edge of a gaping crevasse and peered in. The pale blue of the icy walls stretched down and down into darker depths of inky blue and black. They shouted to Ninnis. The wail of an injured dog could be heard rising faintly out of the abyss. But no human sound came in response to their calls.

As the hours passed they called and begged Ninnis to reply. They lowered their longest rope into the crevasse but it didn't even reach the narrow ledge where the injured dog lay. They stared into the murky depths through binoculars. Finally, the full horror of the situation became apparent. Ninnis was dead, or worse, still alive and slowly dying.

Their own situation was now desperate. The sledge which had plunged into the crevasse with Ninnis was loaded with all the dog rations, all but a week's supply of their own food, their tent and groundsheet, Mertz's waterproof pants and hat, the pick-axe, spade and other vital pieces of equipment. And they were 320 miles from Cape Denison. Mawson read the funeral service at the edge of the crevasse, and at 9 p.m. they set off on the long journey back.

At 2:30 a.m. they made a rough tent from a light tarpaulin and spare sledge-runners, fed the dogs a meal of old boots and gloves, and slept, no doubt uneasily.

Soon they were both losing strips of skin and hair but they had no idea why.

On waking, Mawson killed the weakest dog. He kept the liver and fatty bits of flesh for himself and Mertz, and tossed the remains to the other dogs. They toiled on, not realizing that eating the fat and healthy-looking dog livers would lead to pain, illness, insanity, and ultimately for Mertz, death. The liver of Greenland huskies contains excessive amounts of vitamin A. There is more than enough of the vitamin in just one liver to kill two men.

Within a week they felt the first symptoms of poisoning: dizziness, nausea, stomach pain and dysentery accompanied by listlessness and irritability. Mertz, without his waterproof pants and hat, suffered more. As they crossed the crevasse-riddled Ninnis Glacier his condition rapidly deteriorated. Soon they were both losing strips of skin and hair but they had no idea why. Mertz half-joked to Mawson, 'I have felt all the time that the diet of a dog does not agree with me.'

Their pace literally slowed to a crawl when Mawson dropped onto all fours and pulled the sledge with Mertz tied on board, who was suffering constantly from pain, dizziness and nausea. By now the dogs were all dead. As each animal became too exhausted to pull, the men had laid its emaciated body on the sledge, carried it along and used it for food. They killed the last one with the spade. The rifle had long since been abandoned.

Mertz was now in the last stages of delirium. 'Am I a man—or a dog?' he yelled at Mawson one night. 'You think I have no courage because I cannot walk. But I show you, I show...' He raised a frostbitten finger to his mouth, and to Mawson's horror, bit into it. For ten seconds or more he gnawed at it, tearing the bone and flesh and groaning all the time, until he finally bit it right off and spat it out on the ground.

The end was near for this intelligent, good-humored man, but he continued to rage violently for another 24 hours. At one stage Mawson had to sit on his chest to stop him damaging the tent. In the middle of the night Mawson awoke to find that Xavier Mertz had died quietly in his sleep. His horrible agony was over, but Mawson's had barely begun.

One piece of dog-liver, a set of paws, 40 biscuits, a few

bits of chocolate and a little dried meat now made up Mawson's menu for the remaining 100 miles. His chance of survival was slim.

Mawson cut the sledge down to half its original size, threw away some fuel and other gear, and started walking. Soon he was crawling. Later he removed his boots and socks and discovered that his soles had almost completely separated from the watery, bloody mush that still served for feet. Relief came in the form of a blizzard, which confined him to his tent for 30 hours. He rested and regained some strength.

The Mertz Glacier was the next obstacle: 12 miles of icy chasms lightly covered and obscured by treacherous bridges of snow. At 3 p.m. on 17 January 1912 the snow gave way beneath his feet and he dropped like a stone. The sledge harness bit deep into his body, causing a flash of agonizing pain, as the 12-foot rope tying him to the sledge jerked him to a halt. Then, as he hung there, the sledge moved, ever so slowly, towards the edge of the chasm and ... stopped.

Mawson looked around. Below, the glassy walls plunged sheer to milky depths. Above was a thin sliver of light, with the quivering rope carved deep into a snowy lip. It took every ounce of his strength to haul himself and the snow that had lodged in his clothes painfully to the top. But when he finally emerged and leaned thankfully on the edge of the crevasse, it broke again and he plunged back to stop with another agonizing jerk at the end of the rope.

Now Mawson was close to despair. Could he endure even more pain and agony? Did he have any strength left to summon? Surely this was the end: his energy was fast ebbing away. He would hang here and die — a frozen corpse suspended forever in the cruelest place on earth.

What makes a person in such dire circumstances continue to fight? As the deadly cold enveloped him, Mawson's unshakable determination came to his rescue and he climbed the rope once more, his hands raw and bleeding, his breath coming in great wheezing gasps, the pain in his body stabbing and throbbing.

He lay in his tent that night unable to sleep, shaking uncontrollably for hour after hour as the glacier boomed and shrieked around him. He knew then that his chances of making it back to base were slipping away. He could not live through another accident. He spent the next day making a rope ladder to replace the safety rope. And the following day he had to use it twice!

Many more crevasses, a lot more despair, and more days confined to his tent by blizzards passed before Mawson emerged from the glacier and climbed the snowy slopes of the last ice dome. At the start of the climb he abandoned more equipment, including his spiked crampons used for walking on ice. This proved a serious mistake because the country ahead of him had less snow covering the ice than he anticipated. His slow pace was constantly interrupted by painful slips and falls.

But now, with his food almost gone, his luck began to change. A strong wind sprang up at his back and he hoisted a 'sail'. Sitting on the sledge he sped across the snow. Later that day he ran slap-bang into a snow-cairn wrapped in black bunting which contained a cache of food!

On 25 January a final search party had left Cape Denison with instructions to return no later than the 30th.

This party had built the cairn when they ran out of time and had to turn back. Also in the cairn was a note giving details of his position and directions back to the ice cave and safety. The note was dated 29 January. They had been there that very day!

At long last Mawson reached the safety of the cave. It was well stocked with food and clothing, but there were no crampons which he desperately needed to walk the icy track to the hut. Outside the blizzard blew for eight days while his physical condition deteriorated. When the weather eventually cleared he ventured out on the slippery walk to safety.

Finally, Mawson rounded a bend in the track. He saw the hut and three people working nearby. He tried to wave and call out, but no one noticed him. At last they saw him and dashed up the slope. Bickerton, the first to reach him, knocked away the ice from his face and stared with horror at his blackened and emaciated features.

'My God,' he murmured, 'which one are you?'

Mawson's normal weight was 209 pounds. On his return to the hut he weighed just 110 pounds.

The relief ship had left Antarctica only six hours earlier. The five men at the hut had volunteered to stay behind for another winter

'My God', he murmured, 'which one are you?'

in case Mawson and his companions returned. Mawson remained gravely ill and severely depressed for many months. Even when the ship returned for them the following summer, he was still haggard and hairless.

He returned to Antarctica eighteen years later but never again attempted a long sledging trip. He died in 1958. One member of the expedition, Eric Webb, described Mawson's journey as 'a triumph of the human spirit over the most formidable adversity'.

Shackleton

One year later, and on the other side of Antarctica, another man was about to test his spirit against that 'most formidable adversity'. That other man was Ernest Shackleton, coming south again in the spring of 1914 to cross the continent on foot.

Before he even reached land, however, Shackleton ran into trouble. On 18 January 1915, still 60 miles from shore, his ship *Endurance* stuck fast in the ice. It was 'frozen', as motor mechanic Orde-Lees put it, 'like an almond nut in the middle of a chocolate bar'. The expeditioners remained on board until 27 October when the ship began to break up under the pressure of the ice.

Ernest Shackleton

On 21 November the ship sank. Shackleton's crew camped nearby waiting for the ice to break up. They were hampered by three heavy lifeboats and huge quantities of food and equipment. When the ice finally did break, they drifted on their floe for three months. On 9 April they took to the boats.

That night, they camped on the iceberg. In the middle of the night, they heard a deafening crack as the floe split in two — right through their camp. They were separated into two groups and one man, still in his sleeping bag, was thrown into the freezing water. Shackleton tore aside a tent and dragged meteorologist Leonard Hussey to safety.

Eventually the party was reunited. Three days later, they reached open water, and headed north for Elephant Island in the South Shetlands. Thanks to the excellent navigational skills of *Endurance* skipper Frank Worsley they reached their destination on 15 April, and surfed ashore in a fierce sea .

Many of the men were now fearfully ill, and some were injured. One man, Perc Blackboro, had chronic frostbite on his toes. The last of the anaesthetic was used to amputate them when gangrene set in.

> **The last of the anaesthetic was used to amputate his toes when gangrene set in.**

At the end of April, Shackleton, Worsely, Thomas Crean (the second officer), and three others set out in the best boat, a 20-foot cutter called the *James Caird*. They made for South Georgia 745 miles away across Drake Passage, the stormiest and most dangerous waterway in the world.

The sun appeared only three times during the voyage, allowing Worsely to navigate, but two weeks later they hit South Georgia with pin-point accuracy. The fourteen days at sea had been accompanied by the deafening roar of the ocean, howling winds, intense cold, and snow. At night the waves breaking over the boat would instantly freeze. Each morning the men had to chip ice off the sail, rigging, mast and gunnels — a dangerous and slippery job. Enormous waves towered 60 feet above them, blocking out all view. The boat would race giddily to the top of each wave like a roller-coaster, then heel over as the wind struck it at the crest. At that moment they could look out over miles of troubled sea, before the boat careered down the other side.

On the eleventh night the wind shifted and Shackleton saw a patch of clear sky in the southwest. He called to the others but as they watched their relief gave way to terror. The clear patch was in fact an enormous wave, perhaps 100 feet high or more, and it was bearing down on their tiny vessel.

It struck the boat like a sledge hammer hitting a cork, tossing it high into the air. Miraculously the boat stayed upright, hit the water again with a crack and shipped water to the gunnels. The men bailed, and the huge 'greybeard', as these freak waves are called, passed on.

By this stage the harrowing conditions were taking their toll. One of the men, Vincent, had fallen into a stunned, inactive stupor. Their water was running low and they still hadn't sighted land.

On the fourteenth day they sighted South Georgia, but the high rocky cliffs offered no easy landing place. They remained offshore all night and at 3 a.m. a violent hurricane struck. The shrieking wind and driving spray propelled them towards the rocks. All next day they fought to keep the boat away and desperately searched for a safe haven, but another night of bitter cold and thirst lay before them.

The following day they finally landed on a little stony beach in the shelter of King Haakon Bay. And to their delight fresh water gurgled down the beach at their feet.

This story of hardship does not end here. Shackleton and his men had yet to climb the mountains, risk the hair-raising toboggan ride described at the beginning of this chapter, climb with the help of ropes down a 50-foot waterfall between vertical walls of rock and then trudge for several more hours into Leith Harbour, before they were rescued. It took them three attempts to rescue their colleagues stranded on Elephant Island.

In terms of its objectives, the expedition was a complete failure, but it is a triumphant story of survival in the face of the most horrifying odds. In his career, Shackleton made three visits to Antarctica; one with Scott and two leading his own expeditions. On all these occasions, all of his men survived. On his fourth journey south, Ernest Shackleton died of a heart attack and was buried on South Georgia Island.

5
Buildings in Antarctica

In 1899 a Norwegian adventurer, Carstens Borchgrevink, an Australian physicist, Louis Bernacchi and eight others became the first people to remain in Antarctica throughout the long, dark winter. The prefabricated pine hut which

Borchgrevink's log cabin at Cape Adare

sheltered them was a sophisticated version of a traditional Norwegian log cabin. It took ten days to erect, and is still standing today, despite the rigors of Antarctic weather and little maintenance over the years.

Ten years later, explorers like Mawson and Scott came with large expeditions, extensive financial backing and more elaborate prefabricated buildings.

Mawson's hut was donated by Sydney timber merchant, George Hudson and Son. It was designed by Mawson and Alfred Hodgeman, and was fully erected in Australia before being dismantled for shipment to Antarctica. Each part was numbered. The eighty-six-foot-square living and sleeping quarters were erected first, on stumps set into holes blasted in the rock. Fifty tons of stones were then placed around the stumps to hold the building down in the fierce winds. A smaller hut was added to the main hut, to act as a workshop, laboratory and generator room. Verandahs on three sides provided storage areas and shelter for the dogs.

Some difficulties were encountered. Cracks in the walls through which driven snow would enter had to be sealed. In the winter the entire building was buried in snow, and a labyrinth of tunnels around the hut provided access, more storage, toilets and garbage disposal. Eventually a trapdoor was cut through the roof. Inside the temperature hovered around 39°F and blankets froze to the walls.

Scott's Cape Evans hut was 50 foot by 20 foot by 10 foot high. The walls were lined inside and out with two layers of boards (four layers in all) and insulated with seaweed packed into a kind of quilt, the forerunner of today's insulation batts. The roof insulation consisted of two layers of boards, 'rubberoid' membrane (a thick rubber

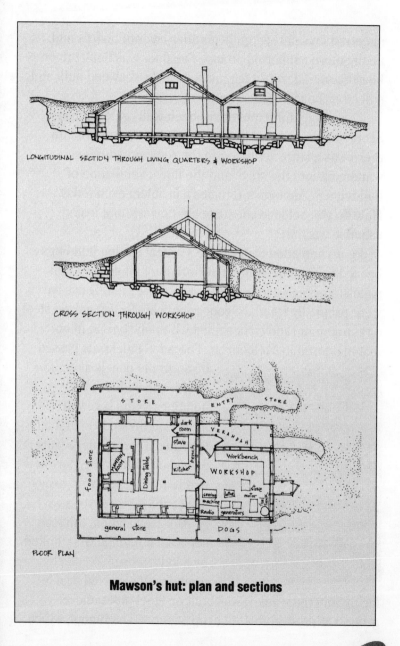

LONGITUDINAL SECTION THROUGH LIVING QUARTERS & WORKSHOP

CROSS SECTION THROUGH WORKSHOP

FLOOR PLAN

Mawson's hut: plan and sections

sheet), then seaweed quilt, another layer of boards and finally more rubberoid on top. The floor was linoleum on boards over a layer of felt, more boards, seaweed quilt and still more boards underneath.

The whole thing must have been well sealed because Scott complained that the hut was 'fuggy', even though there was a large ventilator in the roof and additional vents built into the stove and the flues. Ventilation of buildings in Antarctica remains a problem even today. How do you achieve adequate air-flow without losing valuable warmth?

Poor ventilation in Australia's recent station buildings has led to dampness and deterioration of insulated wall panels. The wall panels at Mawson, Casey and Davis bases were originally standard cool-room panels, galvanized steel or aluminium sandwiches filled with polystyrene foam manufactured in Melbourne. Threaded steel rods passed through the panels along the length and width of the buildings. Nuts screwed tightly on the ends held it all together. The buildings were placed on railway sleepers and tied to the ground with heavy steel cables.

... they only needed to walk 20 yards back along the tunnel towards their bedrooms before their wet hair was frozen solid!

At Casey station, thirteen separate buildings were linked by a long, wormlike, steel tunnel with a curved profile facing into the wind. It was built on steel poles above ground to prevent the build-up of snow. The tunnel, which was not heated or insulated, served only as a corridor and expeditioners report that, after showering, they only needed to walk 20 yards back along the tunnel towards their bedrooms before their wet hair was frozen solid! Altogether the tunnel was over 200 yards long. It became the course for an unruly foot race once a year as part of the midwinter celebrations.

All three Australian Antarctic stations are now being completely rebuilt as part of a program which started in 1985 with a budget of $76.7 million. Extensive wind-tunnel tests showed that bigger buildings produce less snow drift, so the new buildings are all two storeys. They are all on concrete slabs and have 8-inch-thick insulated wall panels. The plumbing pipes are heated to prevent their contents from freezing. The Australian stations are built on exposed rock. In other places this has not been possible, and various attempts have been made to build permanent structures on, or within, the constantly moving ice.

At the British Halley base on the Bruunt Ice Shelf, four generations of buildings have gone up. Rebuilding is periodically required as sections of the ice shelf break off, or the building is crushed within the ice. The 1982 version consisted of two flexible plywood tubes, half cut into the ice and half buried in drift. Each had two levels of living and working space, connected by short corridors. The building took 60 days to assemble from prefabricated sections.

In 1958 the Americans built a permanent station for eighteen people at the South Pole and called it the Amundsen–Scott base. No one had been there since Scott. The whole station was prefabricated and flown in by Globemaster aircraft flying the 525-mile round trip from McMurdo Sound over a period of four weeks. In this coldest of human habitations, 200 gallons of heating oil are burnt every day. Without continually operating ceiling fans, the temperature would be 82°F hotter near the ceiling than at floor level!

> **Without continually operating ceiling fans, the temperature would be 82°F hotter near the ceiling than at floor level!**

Meanwhile, the spartan huts of the heroic age still withstand the impact of the elements. Some of the baltic pine lining boards on Mawson's hut are half an inch than they were 85 years ago, because they have been worn away by the abrasive, snow-laden wind.

Attempts to repair and preserve Mawson's hut have met with little success. A private operation called 'Project Blizzard', which aimed to survey, repair and restore the hut and other buildings, visited in 1984–5 and 1985–6. The team excavated ice and snow from inside the building, inspected its condition, and carefully collected many pieces of equipment and stores still lying around. Although major repairs were needed, they were not given permission to start the work. Attempts by the Australian Antarctic Division to visit the site since then have been frustrated by weather and ice conditions. Private organizations continue to lobby for the preservation of this important part of Australian history. A replica of Mawson's hut is currently under construction in Melbourne to help raise money for another private expedition.

Australia's failure to care for its Antarctic relics is in

stark contrast to the efforts of a New Zealand 'Hut Caretaker Program' which began in 1969. New Zealanders have repaired and restored Scott's hut at Cape Evans and Shackleton's hut at Cape Royds. To step into either is to walk back in time. Sledges and harnesses hang from the ceiling. Shelves are stocked with cans of food, books and clothing. The stove, tables, chairs and bunks are all in their places, exactly as they were left almost a century ago. Regular inspections and basic maintenance are carried out at these places as well as at Borchgrevink's log cabin, Scott's 'Discovery' hut at Hut Point, and a number of other historically significant sites.

6
Of Dogs and Cats and Weasels

Transport in Antarctica

The main difficulty with Antarctica is just getting around
the place! Anyone who has been to a ski resort during the
winter will have some idea of the problems. Walking in soft
snow is hard, tiring work, but it is harder if you're dragging
mountains of food and equipment behind you, wearing
layers and layers of heavy woollen clothing and leaning
into a 60-mile-an-hour gale. Walking or driving a car on icy
surfaces can be dangerous enough, but it is far worse if the
ice has been sculpted by the wind into an endless sea of
sharp crests and hollows, or if you're likely to break
through the surface at any moment and plunge 100 feet
into a crevasse.

Mechanical vehicles experience special problems in
Antarctica's bitter conditions. Extreme cold affects

batteries and freezes cooling systems and lubricants. Wind-driven snow gets through the tiniest of gaps, clogging and icing up engines. The thin air of high altitudes severely reduces engine power just as it quickly exhausts people doing physical work. Even fixing breakdowns can be a painful business when naked skin sticks instantaneously to super-chilled metal surfaces. And finally, visibility is often poor and the weather can change suddenly to blizzard conditions, pinning down the best-equipped expedition for days on end.

For the early Antarctic explorers, Scott, Amundsen, Shackleton and others, transportation problems were life and death issues. The correct or incorrect decisions about transport determined the success or failure of their efforts before they even started.

The Nansen sledge

At least the choice of a sledge was a simple matter. Veteran Arctic explorer Fridtjof Nansen had adapted and improved the traditional Inuit sledge of northern Canada and Alaska. He trained craftspeople in his home city of Oslo to manufacture the 'Nansen sledge' and it was widely used by Arctic and Antarctic explorers from many different countries.

Douglas Mawson took an Australian-made version with him to Cape Denison. About 10 feet long, it had Australian hardwood runners, a lightweight bamboo platform and a short mast and crosspiece for the 'sail'. A light wheel was mounted behind with an odometer for measuring the distance traveled.

The Nansen sledge could be man-hauled, or pulled by dogs, ponies, or vehicles. Each sledge carried up to 500 pounds. Loads included food, animal rations, tents and poles, groundsheets, stove and stove-fuel, cooking utensils, spare clothing, sleeping bags, ropes, harnesses, ice-picks, spades, hammers, ice-nails, firearms, files, repair kits, first-aid boxes and scientific equipment.

Scott's dilemma

While Amundsen was strongly committed to the use of Greenland huskies to pull his sledges, Scott had a more open mind on the subject. He experimented with Siberian ponies, huskies, tractors and man-hauling. He also sought advice from experienced polar explorers. In 1900 he invited Nansen to witness a trial run of three 'motorized sledges' in Norway. When asked his opinion, Nansen replied, 'Myself, I would take dogs, and dogs, and still more dogs! If a dog breaks down, it provides food for other dogs — even for men. But if a motor breaks down, what is it? Just a heap of oily metal in the snow.'

Nansen's words proved accurate. The motorized sledges which Scott sent out ahead of the main party heading for the pole did break down and

Man-hauling

had to be abandoned.

Scott's final decision in favor of man-hauling seems, in retrospect, bizarre. It is said that he found all forms of cruelty to animals deeply distressing. He may also have believed that the trip to the pole would be a more noble achievement if men did it on their own two feet. Whatever his reasons, it was a disastrous decision which cost Scott and his companions their lives.

Heaps of oily metal in the snow

Many of the early explorers were disappointed by the poor performance of their motor vehicles. Shackleton took a car with him on his 1907 expedition, and while it did good work around the base, it was quite hopeless for any purpose further afield.

Mawson took an airplane with him but the wings were destroyed by the wind soon after arrival. The rest of it was put to good use as a makeshift tractor moving supplies and equipment around the Cape Denison base.

The most spectacular failure of all was U.S. Admiral Richard Byrd's *Snow Cruiser*. This 56-foot long,

diesel-powered monster accompanied Byrd on his third
Antarctic expedition in 1939. Its wheels were 10 feet
in diameter and weighed three tons each. A small plane
rode precariously on its roof. Inside were living quarters,
laboratories, a dark room, workshop, wash rooms and
cockpit. Admiral Byrd had high hopes of riding in it all the
way to the Pole. Alas, it was useless. A six-inch ridge of
soft snow was enough to halt the *Snow Cruiser* in its
tracks. It trundled just over two miles from base, not even
as far as Scott's motor-sledges!

By the time Sir Edmund Hillary and Vivian Fuchs
arrived in Antarctica in 1955, the amount of vehicular junk
lying around must have been spectacular: their
Commonwealth Trans-Antarctic expedition left a further
trail of abandoned vehicles and empty fuel drums from one
side of the continent to the other.

They came with a vehicle fleet which sounded more like
a zoo! Five weasels, four cats,
two beavers, one otter as
well as an assortment
of tractors were
liberated at
Shackleton
base on the
Weddell

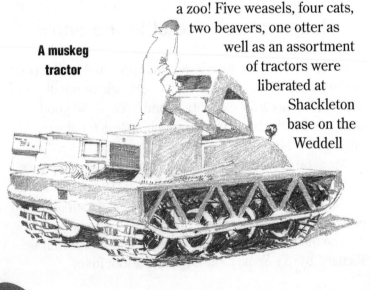

A muskeg tractor

Sea and Scott base on the Ross Sea.

The Weasels were second-hand U.S. army vehicles built during World War II for carrying cargo over difficult terrain. Their traction system consisted of a conventional caterpillar track along each side of the vehicle. Steering was achieved by braking one track only (the inside one) while continuing to drive the other. They were equipped with a straight-six Studebaker engine and had a cruising speed of 8 to 13 miles per hour. It was intended that, as the fuel was used up during the Antarctic crossing, the loads to be dragged along would lessen, and vehicles which broke down could be abandoned along the way. The Weasels were brought along with this in mind.

The glamour vehicles were the four Sno-cats. Made by the U.S. Tucker Sno-Cat Company as personnel and cargo carriers, they were 20 feet long and just over six foot wide. They boasted a maximum speed of 15 miles per hour and guzzled between 40 and 90 gallons of fuel per 60 miles! Their great strength was their unique and very effective traction system. They had four independent caterpillar tracks designed for maximum grip on both ice and snow, each on its own separate 'pon-toon'. Each pontoon could swivel independently, allowing the Sno-Cat to be steered while maintaining forward traction on all four pontoons. Sno-cat cabins were double-glazed, insulated and heated, a far cry from the conditions endured by Mawson and Scott only 50 years earlier.

One thing had not changed however. Crevasses were an ever-present danger, and in heavy vehicles the chances of breaking through a snow bridge were much greater. In crevassed areas the Fuchs–Hillary expedition spent many hours probing the snow ahead with thin poles to find out if it was firm enough to drive on. Vehicles were also roped together, like climbers, so that if one fell into a crevasse, the others could pull it out. And such accidents did occur.

On one occasion, a Sno-cat nicknamed *Rock 'n Roll* by its driver broke through the snow into a 16-foot wide crevasse. When the two occupants opened their doors they saw that the front pontoons had pivoted 90° to rest vertically against the wall of the crevasse. Below them was a 65-foot drop to the first ice shelf. The rear pontoons were still half supported on firm snow. Exit from the driver's side was out of the question. On the passenger side, the men could just stretch out enough to get onto the rear pontoon and then crawl carefully to safety.

Two Sno-cats were brought in side by side and attached with heavy steel cable to the towing hook on the rear of the stranded *Rock 'n Roll*. After finding a safe way over the crevasse, two Weasels took up positions in front, also attached with heavy cables. The Sno-cats then pulled *Rock 'n Roll* out backwards while the Weasels pulled hard enough to stop the front from sliding down into the crevasse. Even then, a cable from another vehicle had to be attached to one of the pontoons to pull it back into its normal position so it wouldn't catch on the lip of the crevasse. A man was lowered down the crevasse on a rope to attach this cable. The whole operation took five hours.

On another occasion Sno-cat *Able* dropped right into a crevasse and came to a halt wedged firmly between the two walls. Only the front of the front pontoons and the top of the rear doors were touching the ice. Luckily there was a snow bridge about 25 feet down and everyone got to

A Sno-cat in trouble

work with shovels filling the rest of the crevasse with snow. Using this snow as a working platform, they inserted crevasse 'bridges' under *Able*'s pontoons.

The bridges were 13-foot-long aluminium planks carried with the expedition for this purpose. They were supported on ledges cut into the crevasse walls and by steel cables running back to firmly embedded timber posts. Once all this was done, two cats pulled the stranded one out forwards, while two Weasels secured the back in case the bridging collapsed.

Despite these problems, the Commonwealth Trans-Antarctic expedition covered the 2,156 miles from Shackleton to Scott base in 99 days, averaging 22 miles a day. The maximum day's run was 72 miles.

Aircraft in Antarctica

The first person to fly an airplane in Antarctica was an Australian, Hubert Wilkins. In November 1928 he flew a Lockheed Vega from Deception Island along the length of the Antarctic Peninsula and back again. This was followed by more exploratory flights the following year.

Wilkins was an extraordinary individual who deserves more fame than the history books have given him. Born in outback South Australia, he trained as an engineer when his family was forced off the land by years of drought. His lifetime of adventure, achievement and heroism included numerous expeditions to both the Arctic and Antarctic. As well he worked as an anthropologist among the Aboriginal people of northern Australia, filmed the Western Front during World War I, spied for the Americans during World War II, and worked as both a naturalist and a pilot. Amongst his many other interests he found time to conduct experiments in mental telepathy! Sir John Monash described him as 'the bravest man I ever saw'.

Admiral Richard Byrd had more luck with flying machines than with his *Snow Cruiser*! He and three others were the first to fly to the South Pole and back in their three-engined Fokker Friendship, the *Floyd Bennett*. In the thin air over the Antarctic plateau, the aircraft was unable to fly high enough to cross the mountains. Two 125-pound bags of food (their entire emergency rations) went overboard to lighten the plane. Had they been forced down they would certainly have starved to death long before help could reach them.

7
Adventures in Science

Although the lure of adventure still draws many to its icy shores, Antarctica now holds little for the kind of resourceful amateurs who joined the early expeditions. Today it is the domain of scientists and technicians, and research is the name of the game. But what is it about Antarctica that is so fascinating for scientists?

The weather

Not the most fascinating topic in the world you may think, but for meteorologists, Antarctica is where it's at. Both polar regions have a powerful influence on worldwide weather conditions. Mawson proposed in 1911 that a permanent weather station in Antarctica would provide better weather forecasting for ships using oceans to the south of Australia and New Zealand. Today's

75

understanding of Antarctic weather and the constant monitoring made possible by 25 permanent meteorological stations have greatly improved weather forecasting the world over.

Antarctica also holds important clues about past and future weather patterns. Samples of ice drilled from deep in the ice cap have provided information on the climate up to half a million years ago. They also show us that the chemical composition of the atmosphere has altered and that these alterations have been particularly dramatic in the last hundred years. They indicate that the average temperature of the world's atmosphere has risen by almost one and a half degrees in the past twenty years. Most scientists believe that this trend is likely to continue.

Samples of ice drilled from deep in the ice cap indicate that the average temperature of the world's atmosphere has risen by almost one and a half degrees in the past twenty years.

The discovery of a hole in the ozone layer in 1981 by British scientists working in Antarctica, and more recent monitoring of its increasing size have caused alarm among scientists worldwide. The layer of ozone in the atmosphere, about 30 miles above the earth's surface, helps to filter out dangerous ultraviolet rays from the sun. The 'hole' or thinning of this layer over Antarctica has been caused by chemicals called *chlorofluorocarbons*, and other gases used in refrigerators, air-conditioners, polystyrene packaging and other manufactured items. There are now international agreements to phase out the manufacture of these damaging materials.

Auroras

The Maoris called them 'Tahu-Nui-A-Rangi' or 'the great burning of the sky'. Few photos or paintings do them justice, but all who witness auroras are spellbound by their beauty.

The northern lights (Aurora Borealis) occurring near the North Pole, and the Southern lights (Aurora Australis) near the South Pole are caused when an unsteady stream of electrically charged particles from the sun is trapped in the earth's magnetic field, causing the existing gases to heat up and glow, rather like the neon gas in a fluorescent light.

They occur anywhere from 50 to 620 miles up, and their colour depends on the height and on the particular gases involved. They are at their strongest and most brilliant during spring and autumn and during the magnetic storms following solar flares (huge thermo-nuclear explosions on the surface of the sun). They are associated with enormous amounts of electrical energy.

Magnetics

The magnetic field of the earth is responsible for the wondrous beauty of the auroras. It is also a major factor in map-making and navigation.

Navigation, even today, is partly dependent on magnetic compasses showing the direction of the North and South magnetic poles. The problem is that the magnetic poles keep moving around in response to huge movements of molten rock deep within the earth. The South Geographic Pole (the one the early explorers all wanted to get to first) is a fixed position and all maps are drawn in relation to this spot. It is important therefore, that we know accurately from year to year the position of the wandering magnetic pole relative to the fixed geographic pole. Detailed magnetic observations by the early explorers over long periods of time were aimed at carefully checking the exact position of the magnetic pole, and trying to make sense of its arbitrary drift.

Geology

Wherever people go, they seem to want to dig bits of the earth up and sell them. Geology is the science of seeing

Mineral-bearing rock in the Theron Mountains

whether there's anything there worth digging up. Mawson himself was a geologist by profession.

And, yes there *are* minerals buried under the snow and ice of Antarctica, and no doubt they lie at the heart of so much international interest in the place. So far, however, the climate and other practical difficulties involved in mining Antarctica have made geology a purely academic exercise there.

Of more interest to many geologists is the number of meteorites in Antarctica. Mawson's 1912 expedition came across the first of what has proven a treasure trove of extra-terrestrial objects. The ice melting around these hot rocks, and then solidifying again has preserved them intact, so many of the meteorites that land here are eventually found before they can break up or weather away. Many rare and unusual meteorites have been recovered in Antarctica.

The ice has also preserved a number of other fascinating objects. Whole petrified tree trunks left over from the forests of Gondwanaland were found in the Queen Adelaide Range in 1967, together with some fossils that were 200 million years old. One was the jaw bone of a giant salamander.

Glaciology

The ice itself has been the subject of considerable scientific interest. How thick is it? How fast is it moving? How much water is locked up here? Each spring, expeditions from Australia's Casey Base head out to measure the eastern Antarctic's ice thickness and rate of flow. They are on the ice for four months every summer, accumulating masses of information.

Human physiology

The ability of human beings to survive in the harsh conditions of Antarctica remains an abiding fascination for all who go there. The dominant factor is food. The success of all Antarctic exploration, even today, is dependent on the right amounts of different kinds of food being available to provide energy for the work involved, and to maintain body heat when the temperature is very low. Even in comfortable conditions, more than half the food we eat is used up just to maintain body heat. The colder the environment, the more food is used just for this purpose. Additional food, of course, is needed to supply energy for strenuous physical work. People working at the South Pole station, for example, require 5,000 calories a day, compared with the 3,500 calories needed by a manual worker under normal conditions. During a recent British man-hauling expedition which crossed the continent from one side to the other, two men each consumed 10,000 calories per day.

For man-hauling, the problem has always been that the more food you need, the heavier the load you must drag behind you; the heavier the load you drag, the more food you need. If you get your calculations wrong, you end up in a vicious circle leading to starvation.

The early explorers were aware of this equation, but there were a few dietary subtleties that they did not understand. Their ideas about scurvy, for example, were a long way from the truth. Even Captain Cook in the 1770s appeared to have a very clear understanding that scurvy is caused by not eating enough vitamin C. His three voyages of discovery with their long isolated periods at sea were an ideal laboratory for testing his theories, which were proved to be right. By the late nineteenth century, however, the experts developed other theories—that scurvy was caused by tainted meat, or could be avoided by eating plenty of fresh meat. Up to a point the latter theory is correct. Fresh meat does contain some vitamin C, but not nearly enough to maintain health.

Scott, Shackelton, Mawson and others took very little vitamin C with them on their long sledging trips, and scurvy was a constant problem for them.

The painful blisters of frostbite

The Scott expedition's supply of 35,000 cigars indicates another little health matter that was poorly understood at the time but very relevant to Antarctic conditions. These days we all know that smoking can adversely affect blood-flow in the veins and arteries. When people suffer severe frostbite repeatedly, gangrene will eventually set in if sufficient blood supply is not available to aid the healing process.

The Cruelest Place on Earth

Today a great deal of physiological experimentation is taking place to test people's ability to cope with extreme cold, isolation, and continuous contact with a small group of other people for months on end.

8
People, Pollution and Politics in Antarctica

When Captain Scott advertised for suitably qualified people to join his second Antarctic expedition, there were 8,000 applications. Most expeditions since then have been similarly inundated with applicants, such is the fascination that this bleak, beautiful place holds for all sorts of people.

Thousands have now visited Antarctica. Some have stayed there during the long cold winter, a few for a good many winters. Most countries take an interest in Antarctica and some maintain permanent bases there for scientific purposes. In 1989 there were 44 bases occupied all year round and another 45 occupied only in summer. The total summer population was 2,700 people, of whom 800 stayed for the winter.

Today's luxurious bases have little in common with the bleak outposts of the 'heroic' age. Indeed, some are so big they are more like small towns. By the 1970s, America's

McMurdo Station had accommodation for 800. Now it is even bigger, and has a church, clubs, bars, a picture theatre and four enormous three-storey barracks clad in ugly brown pebble-dash panels. During the summer of 1986–7 a total of 1,500 Americans were working in Antarctica.

Argentina is another country with a heavy involvement in Antarctica. Its main base, a frontier town called Marambio, has an airstrip, 30 buildings and a large permanent population of men, women and children. One child was even born there: in 1970 Emilio Marcos Palma became the first Antarctican!

> **One child was even born there: in 1970 Emilio Marcos Palma became the first Antarctican!**

(The first child in Antarctica was American boy scout, Paul Siple, who accompanied Admiral Byrd's 1929 expedition.)

It is only recently that women have been given any sort of role to play in Antarctica. The first to stay all winter was an American, Dr. Michelle Raney, who stayed at the Scott–Amundsen Base at the South Pole in 1979. She overcame considerable opposition to achieve this. One of the conditions placed on her was that she should regularly rotate her companions at meal times!

The first Australian woman to stay all winter was Dr. Louise Holiday who spent the winter of 1989 at Davis Base, while the first woman to lead any winter party in Antarctica was Australian Diana Patterson who took charge of the 26 people at Mawson Base during the winter of 1989.

Unfortunately, women remain a small minority in Antarctica, and some countries still maintain a male-only policy on the bases!

For the vast majority of us, our only chances of getting to Antarctica are as tourists. The potential of the place as a tourist destination was recognized years ago by U.S. Navy Rear-Admiral David Tyree, who wanted to carve a jet-runway out of the Taylor Dry Valley and build a tourist hotel there. Thank goodness nothing came of that idea. Sight-seeing flights over Antarctica operated for several years but ended in 1979 when an Air New Zealand DC 10 crashed into Mount Erebus, killing all 257 passengers and crew. More recently, luxury ships have cruised Antarctic waters, allowing the passengers ashore to visit some of the historic sites as well as the currently occupied bases.

While allowing an increasing number of people to see and appreciate the majesty of Antarctica, tourist operations also have their problems. Accidents in this inhospitable environment usually have fatal consequences. Rescue operations are at best expensive, at worst impossible. In addition, pollution and disturbance of the delicate web of life in Antarctica can also be disastrous. A big reduction in the population of a penguin rookery at Cape Royds has been blamed on large numbers of visits by both tourists and scientists. More recently, a series of reserves has been established in such places, but they are not policed. Internationally agreed guidelines covering these special areas are largely ignored.

In 1983, for example, three small islands that lie in a straight line near an emperor penguin rookery were flattened by blasting to make an 360-feet long landing strip for the French government. Likewise, Australia's newest buildings at Casey station have been built almost on top of rich colonies of moss, lichens and algae in an internationally protected area.

Right from the start, the environmental impact of human beings on Antarctica has been a shameful business. The early explorers left a trail of cookie tins, cigarette butts, sledges and equipment behind them. No attempt was made to collect or dispose of garbage or damaged equipment. More recently, large numbers of vehicles, aircraft and thousands of empty fuel drums have been dumped. The Commonwealth Trans-Antarctic expedition of 1955–8 (see chapter 6) left a string of broken-down vehicles and empty fuel drums extending from one side of the continent to the other. The wreck of a U.S. helicopter still lies in the Wright Dry Valley years after the crash happened, and Admiral Byrd's Fokker monoplane, wrecked in the Rockefeller Mountains can still also be seen. Crevasses have been routinely used for dumping human waste or other garbage. Oily old bits of machinery often end up in the sea resulting in the biological death of some areas of the sea bed.

Toxic pollution has also found its own way to Antarctica from the outside world. Adélie penguin eggs and fat reveal traces of DDT

> **Toxic pollution has also found its own way to Antarctica from the outside world. Adélie penguin eggs and fat reveal traces of DDT and radioactive substances.**

Fuel drums in the snow

and radioactive substances
such as Krypton 85. Ice cores
taken from glaciers show dramatic
increases in radiation following large-scale atmospheric
testing of nuclear weapons.

And there's plenty of Australian garbage in Antarctica.
When Wilkes base was abandoned in favor of the new Casey
base in 1969, the garbage dump there included machine
parts, bottled food and 200 boxes containing tins of caustic
soda, some of them leaking. The new base's open garbage
dump, used from 1969 to 1984, contains over 15,000 cubic
yards of rubbish. Large numbers of birds attracted to the
food waste are also at risk from the toxic chemicals lying
around. The Australian Antarctic Division is about to begin a
ten-year operation to bring all that garbage home.

Another completely new base has now been built at
Casey. The 1969 base, thirteen buildings connected by an
aerodynamic 'tunnel' (see chapter 5), has now been cut up

and brought back to the Hobart dump. These days, most of the bases in Antarctica, including Casey and Australia's other brand-new bases, look very much like messy industrial estates.

In the 1960s a U.S. nuclear reactor was built very close to the foot of Mount Erebus (an active volcano!). It lasted for ten years, its operations punctuated by fires, shut-downs, and radioactive leaks. Eventually it was dismantled and shipped back to the U.S. together with a hundred large drums of radioactive earth. Later, more than 14,000 cubic yards of radioactive soil and rock were shipped out. Six more years of clean-up work followed before the area was declared to have 'decontamination levels as low as reasonably achievable'.

Many countries claim parts of Antarctica. Some of these claims conflict and very few are recognized by anyone else. In 1959, twelve countries with an interest in Antarctica signed a treaty 'freezing' all claims, while not recognizing any of them. The treaty proclaims Antarctica as a non-military zone (although many national research efforts there are conducted almost entirely by the military), bans nuclear explosions, allows freedom of access for all, and preserves it for peaceful scientific purposes. Other countries have since joined the treaty, but the issue of territorial claims remains unresolved.

A proposal to declare Antarctica a World Park in which most commercial activities would be banned has slowly but surely gathered momentum over the last few years. It currently enjoys the support of many environmental groups and several governments including those of

Australia and France. Others like Japan oppose it because of their wish to resume full-scale commercial whaling. Another proposal to create a Whale Sanctuary in the oceans around Antarctica was considered by the International Whaling Commission in 1994. Many small countries were persuaded to join the commission by pro-whaling countries in an effort to defeat the proposal, but on 26 May 1994, the sanctuary was agreed to.

It is only fitting that the last word should go to Sir Peter Scott, who was just two years old when his father died in Antarctica: 'I believe we should have the wisdom to know when to leave a place alone.'

GLOSSARY

blizzard: a violent windstorm with dry, driving snow and intense cold, or a heavy snowstorm

cairn: a pile of stones or snow set up as a landmark

crampons: spiked iron plates worn on shoes to ensure a grip on slippery surfaces such as snow

crevasse: a fissure or deep cleft in the ice of a glacier

frostbite: inflammation or gangrene on a part of the body, caused by exposure to intense cold

gangrene: the dying of body tissue, usually caused by the circulation being interrupted

Gondwanaland: an ancient continent which included India, Australia, Antarctica and part of Africa and South America in Palaeozoic and Mesozoic times

husky: a strong dog used in a team to pull sledges over the snow

iceberg: also known as floes. A large floating mass of ice, detached from a glacier and carried out to sea, or formed on the surface of the sea

invertebrate: an animal that doesn't have a backbone

meteorite: a mass of stone or metal which has reached the earth from outer space

meteorology: the science dealing with the atmosphere and its phenomena, especially the weather

scurvy: a disease caused by a lack of Vitamin C which results in swollen and bleeding gums, liver spots on the skin, pain in the limbs, and general illness

South Pole: the end of the earth's axis of rotation, marking the southernmost point of the earth. The South Geographic Pole is a fixed point and all maps are drawn in relation to this fixed spot. The South Magnetic Pole is the point given by a compass when it points to 'south'. However this pole actually moves in response to huge movements of molten rock far below the earth's surface.

Yankee sealers and whalers: Yankee seafarers in general have a special place in the history of nineteenth-century sailing. North American or Yankee skippers were hard, tough sailors who took tremendous risks to achieve fast passages and ruled their ships with their bare fists. Yankee ships were reputed to be sleeker and faster than their traditional European counterparts.

FURTHER READING

If you would like to find out more about Antarctica, the following list should help you. Most of the books should be available in public libraries; if not, ask your librarian to get them in for you.

This Accursed Land
by L. Bickel
(Macmillan, Melbourne, 1977)

Whales of the World
by N. Bonner
(Facts on File, New York, 1989)

Going to Extremes
by J. Chester
(Doubleday, Sydney, 1986)

Antarctica — The Heroic Age
by G. Finkel
(Collins, Sydney, 1976)

The Crossing of Antarctica
by V. Fuchs and E. Hillary
(Cassell, London, 1958)

Scott of the Antarctic
by E. Huxley
(Weidenfeld & Nicholson, London, 1977)

The Greenpeace Book of Antarctica
by J. May
(Dorling Kindersley, London, 1988)

A History of Polar Exploration
by J. Mountfield
(Hamlyn, London, 1976)

INDEX